1

Purpose

Presidential Policy Directive 18 (PPD-18)[1] established United States Government policy on Maritime Security and provided for the development of scalable, flexible frameworks on specific maritime issues to guide and clarify roles and responsibilities for strategic goals of the United States. This document:

- Affirms the vital national interest in global maritime security and articulates United States Government policy for countering piracy, robbery at sea, and related maritime crime;
- Provides the overarching guidance to develop objectives to enhance maritime security in other regions of the world as required based on evolving and emerging threats; and
- Supersedes the Countering Piracy off the Horn of Africa: Partnership and Action Plan[2].

Background and Overview

This Plan implements the National Strategy for Maritime Security[3] (Strategy) and the Policy for the Repression of Piracy and other Criminal Acts of Violence at Sea[4] (Policy). The Strategy affirms the vital national interest of the United States in maritime security and recognizes that nations have a common interest in achieving two complementary objectives: facilitating the vibrant maritime commerce that underpins economic security; and protecting against piracy, robbery at sea, and related maritime crime.

Our Policy provides that we shall "continue to lead and support international efforts to repress piracy . . . and urge other States to take decisive action both individually and through international efforts."[5] Through this Plan, the United States will seek to involve all nations, international organizations, industry, and other entities that have an interest in maritime security to take steps to repress piracy and related maritime crime. An integrated and comprehensive approach, through international coordination and cooperation, will advance objectives that enhance the global economy and promote freedom of the seas.

The nations of the world have long considered pirates to be universal enemies of mankind. Under customary international law, as reflected in the 1982 Law of the Sea Convention, every nation has jurisdiction to prosecute a suspected pirate for the crime of piracy, regardless of any connection between the State and the suspected pirate, the vessel, or the victims. Our interdependent and interconnected global society revolves around a world economy that depends upon maritime shipping. Governments must collaborate with international organizations and the shipping industry to confront and repress any persistent threat to global commerce.

---

[1] PPD-18 Maritime Security, August 14, 2012, which reaffirms the 2005 National Strategy on Maritime Security and establishes issue-related Maritime Frameworks, one of which is piracy off the Horn of Africa.

[2] National Security Council Countering Piracy off the Horn of Africa: Partnership & Action Plan, December 2008.

[3] National Strategy on Maritime Security, 2005.
[4] Policy for the Repression of Piracy and other Criminal Acts of Violence at Sea, June 2007.
[5] Id

Piracy and related maritime crime continue to plague mariners throughout the world and will continue to pose obstacles to the lawful use of the maritime domain. Due to changing conditions around the world, this Plan and its annexes will be periodically reviewed and updated to reflect United States Government policy regarding countering piracy and related maritime crime. As required, scalable, flexible annexes will be developed to address regional maritime criminal activities and coordinate U.S. and international policies to prevent, suppress, and prosecute these crimes effectively.

Flag, victim, and coastal States all have a stake in repressing piracy and related maritime crime. The United States will continue to foster international cooperation and integration among nations, international organizations, and industry, and to support and encourage affected States to exercise jurisdiction, including efforts to build justice-sector capacities. The United States will provide appropriate investigative and logistical support and assistance to other foreign States involved in response to acts of piracy and related maritime crime. When appropriate, the United States will prosecute persons or entities involved in piracy and related maritime crime.

Strategic Vision

The United States will use all appropriate instruments of national power to repress piracy and related maritime crime. The United States will seek to strengthen regional governance and rule of law to maintain the safety and security of mariners, preserve freedom of the seas, and promote the free flow of commerce through lawful economic activity.

Policy Priorities

The United States will continue to be a leader in combating piracy and related maritime crime. The United States, like most nations, relies heavily on international trade, secure global navigation, and unhindered legitimate commerce. Piracy and related maritime crime endanger ocean commerce and transportation, interfere with freedom of the seas, impede the lawful flow of commerce, and undermine regional stability.

Piracy and related maritime crime endanger maritime interests on a global scale, and countering this threat is a shared global responsibility. The United States will continue to collaborate with States and international and regional organizations, including the maritime industry and non-governmental organizations, to develop greater resources and authorities to combat piracy and related maritime crime, and maximize the coordination of our efforts.

Combating piracy and related maritime crime requires the judicious use of all the tools of national power, including diplomatic, economic, social, military, intelligence, law enforcement, and judicial measures. A decisive and effective response to criminal activity and its perpetrators sends an important message of deterrence but requires coordination among all departments and agencies of the United States Government, as well with international partners. The primary efforts of the United States should focus on preventive actions, interruption of piracy acts, and building maritime security and governance capacity in affected States to hold pirates accountable.

It is the policy of the United States to repress piracy and related maritime crime, consistent with national law and international obligations, and to collaborate with other nations in this effort. The United States Government will:

- Reduce the vulnerability of the maritime domain to piracy and related maritime crime;

- Prevent pirate attacks and related maritime crime against U.S. vessels, persons, and interests, as well as those of our allies and partners;

- Interrupt and terminate acts of piracy and related maritime crime consistent with international law and the rights and responsibilities of coastal, flag, and other States;

- Ensure that those who commit acts of piracy and related maritime crime are held accountable for their actions by facilitating the prosecution of suspected pirates and ensure that persons committing maritime crime are similarly held accountable by regional, flag, victim, or littoral States or, in appropriate cases, the United States;

- Preserve the freedom of the seas, including all the rights, freedoms, and uses of the sea recognized in international law;

- Protect ocean commerce and transportation;

- Continue to lead and support international efforts to combat piracy and related maritime crime and urge other States to take decisive action both individually and through international efforts;

- Build the capacity and political will of regional States to combat piracy and related maritime crime, focusing in particular on creating institutional capacity for governance and the rule of law; and

- Strengthen national law to better enable successful prosecution of all members of piracy-related criminal enterprises, including those involved in financing, negotiating, or otherwise facilitating acts of piracy or related maritime crime.

Although overarching policy priorities remain the same, the ways and means to respond to threats will vary according to geographic, political, and legal environments. The annexed frameworks will establish the tailored and specific methodology for different regions, but will focus on three primary areas: Prevention of Attacks, Response to Acts of Maritime Crime, and Enhancing Maritime Security and Governance.

Implementation
The Maritime Security Interagency Policy Committee, or its successor, will lead the interagency process to accomplish the following tasks:

- Oversee the development and implementation of maritime frameworks for the preventive actions and response by the United States Government to piracy and related maritime crime that threaten the safety of the global maritime transportation system, framed on the following principles:
  - Prevention of Attacks – The first and best defense against piracy and related maritime crime, as shown through best management practices, is to reduce the vessel's risk and susceptibility to attack and to be prepared for a potential assault. Industry, ship owners,

and mariners that operate in high-risk regions are best situated to prepare vessels before an attack occurs.

- Response to Acts of Maritime Crime – Piracy and related maritime crime must not be ignored. A rapid and effective response will deter future criminal acts. These measures are designed to be implemented by affected mariners, security services, regional or affected nations, and/or international coalitions.
- Enhance Maritime Security and Governance – A lack of shore-side governance and the failure of governments to deploy adequate maritime security measures is a primary factor that allows piracy and related maritime crime to flourish. These objectives are intended primarily for the United States and international partners to facilitate the development of regional governance by States and the adoption of rule of law by their citizens.

- Review existing U.S. laws against or relating to piracy and related maritime crime and, if necessary, prepare for consideration appropriate amendments to those U.S. laws to enhance our ability to prosecute individuals in U.S. courts who commit acts of piracy and related maritime crime, as well as those who aid and abet or otherwise facilitate such acts; and

- Build international cooperation, consistent with the International Outreach and Coordination Strategy of the National Strategy for Maritime Security,[6] to enhance the ability of other States to combat piracy and related maritime crime and to support U.S. counterpiracy actions.

Annex A: **Framework for Combating Piracy and Enhancing Maritime Security off the Horn of Africa**

Annex B: **Framework for Combating Piracy and Enhancing Maritime Security in the Gulf of Guinea**

---

[6] International Outreach and Coordination Strategy, November 2005.

Framework for
Combating Piracy and Enhancing Maritime Security off the Horn of Africa

---

Background

In the early nineties, following the collapse of Somalia's government and economy, Somali-based pirates began attacking vessels and ransoming crews for private gain. Due to its location near the Gulf of Aden, a strategic maritime corridor, these actions greatly influenced maritime transportation routes and operations, costing the global economy about $18 billion dollars in increased trading costs. The lack of regional stability, coupled with corruption, further facilitated the spread of piracy off the Horn of Africa (HOA), as criminals had little disincentive or constraint to discontinue the lucrative practice. The increase in the pirates' wealth led to the expansion of their infrastructure and capacities on land.

Somali piracy involves hijacking vessels and kidnapping crew for ransom. Generally, cargo is not stolen and hostages are rarely killed. The fatalities that do occur are typically a result of severe mistreatment or neglect at the hands of the captors. Hijacked ships and crew are held as long as necessary to obtain financial payoffs, in many cases for years. A single pirate attack can affect the interests of numerous countries, including the flag State of the vessel, the nations represented by those seafarers taken hostage, regional coastal States, as well as the nation-States of the vessel owners, of the cargo destination, and of the transshipment locations.

Nearly 12 percent of the world's petroleum passes through the Gulf of Aden, one of the world's most important waterways. Pirate attacks undermine confidence in global sea lines of communication, weaken or undermine the legitimacy of affected States, threaten the legitimate revenue and resources essential to the rebuilding of Somalia, increase maritime insurance rates and cargo costs, increase the risk of environmental damage, and endanger the lives of seafarers who may be injured, killed, or taken hostage by pirates for ransom.

The international community, with strong leadership by the United States, has made great strides since 2008 in countering piracy off the HOA. Through the concerted efforts of the international Contact Group on Piracy off the Coast of Somalia (CGPCS), piracy off the HOA has dropped to its lowest levels since 2006. Yet, maritime piracy emanating from the under-governed shores of Somalia still threatens maritime trade in this strategically vital region of the world. The conditions that allowed piracy to flourish still exist in Somalia today. Most of the pirate criminal networks and their shore-based infrastructure likely remain intact. This annex implements the U.S. policy to foster international cooperation and integration among all nations, international organizations, industry, and other entities that have an interest in maritime security to ensure the full range of lawful and timely actions necessary to combat piracy and criminal activity off the HOA.

Overview of the Threat

Somali piracy involves hijacking vessels and kidnapping crew and passengers for ransom. Pirates attack targets of opportunity in the Red Sea, the Gulf of Aden, the Gulf of Oman, and the

Indian Ocean. Typically, pirates armed with small arms and rocket-propelled grenades use outboard powered skiffs to approach and board slower moving commercial vessels. Once onboard, pirates typically can capture the crew and commandeer a vessel in less than 20 minutes. If the hijacked vessel is of low ransom value, such as a fishing vessel or cargo dhow, pirates may use it as a "mother ship" to launch additional attacks farther from the coast on larger, more lucrative merchant vessels.

Ransom payments are the lifeblood of Somali pirate networks, which have evolved their organized transnational criminal enterprises to include other illegal activities and expanded criminal networks. Somali pirates[1] have been paid hundreds of millions of dollars in ransom, funding more attacks and other forms of criminal activity in the region. Overall, piracy and related maritime crime in this region costs the international community billions of dollars annually.[2]

Pirate attacks emanating from Somalia are now at the lowest levels since 2006, due primarily to the following factors:

- Proactive and coordinated naval action by ships of the Combined Maritime Forces' Combined Task Force-151, NATO's OPERATION OCEAN SHIELD, and European Union Naval Forces' OPERATION ATALANTA, as well as by the national naval forces of other nations, including China, Indonesia, India, and Russia;

- Adherence by commercial vessels to industry-developed Best Management Practices[3] (BMP) and the increased use of embarked armed security teams;

- Increasing will of affected States to prosecute piracy — more than 1,400 pirates are now held in more than 20 States; and

- Improving stability in Somalia, including the creation of a new provisional constitution, new parliament, and a new presidency to support effective and responsible governance to combat the nation's social, legal, economic, and operational challenges.

Due to the success of the international community against piracy and related maritime crime off the HOA, there is the potential for the maritime industry to relax its use of BMP and to reduce overhead costs by sailing without privately contracted armed security personnel (PCASP) in High Risk Waters or by using substandard PCASP. Under the existing uneven international regulatory regime, this could result in undesirable consequences including: erosion of BMP implemented by masters, thereby increasing the likelihood of an attack; undesirable uses of force; or a successful attack by pirates against a vessel protected by substandard PCASP. Additionally, international coalitions may seek to reduce the scope and scale of counter-piracy operations as the threat appears to diminish. However, the decline in incidents does not

---

[1] http://oceansbeyondpiracy.org/sites/default/files/documents_old/The_Economic_Cost_of_Piracy_Full_Report.pdf.
[2] Ibid.
[3] Best Management Practices for Protection Against Somalia Based Piracy, Version 4 printed August 2011, ISBN: 978 1 85609 5051.

necessarily imply a reduction in the threat to vessels transiting through the HOA. Although many of those involved in financing and leading pirate attacks have temporarily moved on to other ventures, pirate groups remain operational. Suspicious approaches continue to be reported in the Arabian Sea, the Indian Ocean, the southern Red Sea, the Gulf of Aden, and the Gulf of Oman. In addition, Somali pirates retain the capability to target vessels at great distances from the Somali coast, highlighting the importance of continued caution and the potential danger of complacency.

The basic conditions that permitted piracy to flourish in the first place – a lack of effective control by legitimate security forces of the littoral and maritime areas of Somalia, a poor economy, a lack of regional governance and corruption, and inadequate legal consequences — have improved over the last few years, but significant improvements are still required. A reduced commitment by naval counter-piracy force providers or diminished self-protection measures by commercial shipping likely will result in a resurgence of successful hijackings. There appears to be a growing awareness among Somalis themselves of the toxic effect piracy and related maritime crime has on their communities. Proactive prosecution and long prison sentences have directly challenged the impression of impunity for this crime. As a result, pirates have been pushed out of some locales along the Somali coast.

Objectives

The paramount goal of the United States is to safeguard U.S. citizens and U.S. interests, including protection of the lawful flow of commerce off the HOA. This will best be accomplished in the maritime domain by repressing Somali piracy through actions by the United States and the international community in the short term and by enabling the Somali government to eventually police its own territory. The United States, in concert with partner nations, international coalitions, and nongovernmental organizations, will continue to focus on the three primary areas of prevention, response, and governance. U.S. departments and agencies, consistent with respective authorities and other national missions and priorities, shall pursue the following objectives.

Prevention of Attacks

The international community, despite its commitment to combating piracy and related maritime crime, cannot effectively patrol the entire region off the HOA. Support by industry and merchant mariners is critical to making the pirate business model unsustainable. Making piracy and related maritime crime an untenable business is best realized by preventing the capture of merchant mariners and commercial vessels in waters under pirate threat, which will significantly hinder financial gains by the criminal enterprise. Specific actions including the following:

- Inform U.S. citizens. Maritime Advisories and Port Security Advisories, which clearly outline regional threats, continue to provide critical guidance on BMP to protect U.S. merchant mariners, ships, and cargo off the HOA. U.S. departments and agencies will work with public-facing elements of the United States Government, such as the Department of State's Bureau of Consular Affairs, the U.S. Coast Guard, and the Department of

Transportation to provide timely threat assessments and warnings for U.S. citizens and companies traveling off the HOA.

- <u>Lead and participate substantively in the ongoing work of the Contact Group on Piracy off the Coast of Somalia,</u> which the United States helped to establish in January 2009 pursuant to U.N. Security Council Resolution 1851.

- <u>Encourage international commercial shipping firms to increase the compliance rate for BMP and harden vessels, including the incorporation of properly trained and equipped armed security.</u> Partner with the shipping industry to improve practical steps merchant ships and crews take to avoid, deter, delay, and counter pirate attacks. The shipping industry's use of BMPs and the increasing use of PCASP are among the measures that continue to be the most effective deterrents against pirate attacks.

- <u>Lead and participate substantively in the Maritime Security Working Group established by the Maritime Safety Committee at the International Maritime Organization (IMO)</u> to provide communication and education in U.S. policies and doctrines involving counter-piracy preventive measures, and to assist in the development of guidelines and recommendations to increase global participation by IMO Member States in counter piracy prevention measures.

- <u>Pursue the implementation of international standards for PCASP,</u> which include an integrated approach to security, planning, training, awareness, documentation, and communication skills.

- <u>Continue industry partnerships,</u> including organizing and participating in workshops with the maritime industry to update, educate, and share information on ways to mitigate the threat of piracy.

<u>Respond to Acts of Maritime Crime</u>

The United States will continue to ensure that pirates do not have easy access or freedom of action in the Indian Ocean, Red Sea, and Gulf of Aden through continued naval and law enforcement support.

- <u>Provide persistent interdiction-capable presence at sea off the HOA.</u> Consistent with other U.S. mission requirements, U.S. Navy and/or U.S. Coast Guard forces operating in the region provide persistent interdiction through presence, conduct maritime counter-piracy operations, and coordinate counter-piracy activities with other forces operating in the region to the extent practicable. When in range, these forces will prevent suspected pirate vessels from operating, respond to reports of pirate attacks with the objective of disrupting such attacks, and, in appropriate circumstances, terminate the act of piracy and any resultant hostage situation with intent to deliver any surviving pirates ashore for prosecution. These forces will also coordinate efforts among all multilateral coalitions such as Combined Maritime Forces, NATO's OPERATION OCEAN SHIELD, the European Union's OPERATION ATALANTA, and independent naval forces.

- <u>Reinforce the longstanding U.S. policy of discouraging the payment of ransoms, prisoner release, policy changes, or other acts of concession</u>. Ransom payments lead to future hijackings of ships at sea, and future hijackings lead to additional ransom payments. Such ransom payments build the capacity of militant and terrorist organizations to conduct attacks.

- <u>Encourage and support international counter-piracy initiatives</u>. The United States will leverage the efforts of various international bodies, such as the Maritime Security Centre – HOA in Northwood, United Kingdom, and the Regional Fusion and Law Enforcement Center for Safety and Security at Sea (REFLECS3) in Victoria, Seychelles, to combat piracy and related maritime crime, share information, build capacity; and Shared Awareness and Deconfliction (SHADE) meetings.

- <u>Disrupt and dismantle pirate bases ashore</u>. Pirates require land-based support and access to weapons to commit acts of violence. Piracy at sea can only be reduced if pirate bases ashore are disrupted or dismantled. U.N. Security Council resolutions confer the authority to take "all appropriate measures" to end piracy, including operations in the littoral and land territory of Somalia. As such, the United States will work with other governments and international organizations to disrupt and dismantle pirate bases to the fullest extent permitted by U.S. and international law.

- <u>Employ criminal investigative capabilities to identify and target the finances of criminals who operate at the higher organizational levels of the piracy enterprise</u>. The piracy model is based on the economic benefits associated with crime. Targeting the finances of the organization and blocking assets of organizational leaders will assist in defeating the criminal enterprise that supports piracy and related maritime crime. The United States will continue to block the assets of certain persons determined pursuant to Executive Order 13536 to have threatened the peace, security, or stability of Somalia through acts of piracy or armed robbery at sea off the coast of Somalia.

- <u>Support and encourage the exercise of relevant and appropriate jurisdiction through the framework of applicable international conventions</u>. In addition to the relevant customary international law on piracy reflected in the 1982 Law of the Sea Convention, the 1979 Hostage Taking Convention, the 1988 Convention on the Suppression of Unlawful Acts Against the Safety of Maritime Navigation, the 2000 Transnational Organized Crime Convention, and the 1999 Terrorist Financing Convention may apply to piracy cases in some circumstances. The United States will fully support and encourage the appropriate exercise of jurisdiction over interdicted pirates in accordance with relevant international law.

<u>Enhance Maritime Security and Governance</u>

Defeating piracy and maritime crime in the long term requires a stable government with a regional population that supports and defends the rule of law. Pirates and those who commit maritime crime flourish under weak governance and cannot function effectively under rule of law. The United States, along with our international partners, will facilitate the development of regional governance by Somalia, including transitional support for prosecution and imprisonment of criminals.

- Promote the re-establishment of governance, security, and economic development in Somalia through the encouragement of political and social will. This objective will take decades, if not generations, to implement. In the meantime, our efforts to combat piracy and related maritime crime will help foster maritime trade security, regional stability, and the recovery of Somalia from two decades of civil war.

- Facilitate, where necessary, the expeditious investigation and prosecution of suspected pirates with lawful and appropriate consequences. It is a key deterrent to piracy and other maritime crime to prosecute individuals who commit these acts and deliver appropriate consequences when there is sufficient evidence. Releasing a suspected pirate without investigation or trial is likely to have little deterrent value for other potential pirates. Conversely, rigorous investigations and convictions with meaningful sentences will reduce the number of active pirates and deter potential recruits. Where U.S. prosecution is not appropriate, we will seek agreements and arrangements with States in the region to facilitate prosecution of suspected pirates.

- Facilitate the development of laws and regulations of States and regional cooperative organizations to combat piracy and related maritime crime. Encourage States, and provide assistance when necessary, to adopt domestic legislation and supporting programs that will permit the effective prosecution of those who commit, incite, or facilitate acts of piracy.

- Develop the investigative and judicial capacities of regional nations. Work bilaterally, and with other interested parties, to identify the nature and scope of international assistance needed to enhance the capacities of States in the region, specifically with respect to the arrest, detention, prosecution, and incarceration of persons involved in piracy and related maritime crime, including arms trafficking and money-laundering to support piracy operations. Promote and assist information-sharing efforts between and among industry, law enforcement, prosecutors, and intelligence professionals to identify and apprehend land-based facilitators in maritime piracy networks.

- Support international and regional efforts to combat transnational organized crime. A significant reason for the decline in piracy acts in the past several years is the African Union Mission in Somalia (AMISOM) efforts to stabilize the region. These efforts have built institutional and operational capacity, disrupted criminal networks, and degraded conditions along the Somali coast that have enabled pirates to operate.

- Establish the regional maritime patrol capacity of Somalia in concert with other capacity-building efforts. Developing the capacity of Somalia to guard and defend its own coast will limit the number of suitable coastal areas available to anchor hijacked ships, making piracy more difficult and less profitable. Partnering with like-minded organizations, such as the European Union's regional Maritime Security Programme (MASE), will address multiple aspects of maritime crime, including piracy, drug and weapon smuggling, human trafficking, illegal fishing, and maritime pollution.

- Educate the Somali government and civilians on the negative effects that piracy and related maritime crime has on communities and economic growth. A robust understanding of how the lack of governance, corruption, and illegal activity detrimentally affect the country's population will engender opposition to criminal enterprises.

Partnerships

International cooperation and integration among regional nations, international organizations, industry, and other entities that have an interest in maritime security and ensuring a full range of lawful and timely actions are necessary to combat piracy and related maritime crime off the HOA.

Most of the world's maritime domain is not subject to the sovereignty or jurisdiction of any single State, and many States do not have the capability or capacity to protect commercial shipping on the high seas, or even within their own territorial seas. International coalitions and partner nations that provide maritime patrol forces contribute to reducing, but cannot provide a complete response to, this threat. An effective response to piracy and related maritime crime requires coordinated and comprehensive multilateral and multi-sectorial cooperation on a global scale with regional focus.

Established in January 2009, the CGPCS has been a remarkably - perhaps uniquely - effective ad hoc construct that brings together stakeholders from governments, international organizations, private industry interests, and charitable, not-for-profit organizations to deliver coordinated solutions to Somali piracy.

Operating independently of, but in close coordination with, the United Nations, the CGPCS is enabled by a series of U.N. Security Council resolutions that recognize and promote its role as the primary coordinator of international efforts to counter Somali piracy. The United States will continue to lead and participate substantively in the work of the CGPCS as it advances our national objectives to combat piracy and develop sustainable efforts that, in the long term, will help to reestablish the rule of law in Somalia.

In addition to cooperation with CGPCS, the United States will continue to lead, support, and collaborate with the efforts of other international organizations including Combined Maritime Force's Coalition Task Force-151, and SHADE meetings.

Implementation, Monitoring, and Review

Successful implementation of these efforts can be measured tangibly by the trends of successful pirate attacks, BMP compliance rates by industry, the percentage of suspected pirates who are prosecuted, and increased maritime security governance and stability within the region. Consideration of intangible benefits may also be evaluated through the Maritime Security Sector Reform Guide[4] created jointly by the Departments of State, Defense, Homeland Security, Transportation, and Justice and the U.S. Agency for International Development.

---

[4] http://www.marad.dot.gov/documents/Maritime_Security_Sector_Reform.pdf

The Counter-Piracy Steering Group (CPSG), consisting of a high-level interagency working group led by the Departments of State and Defense, will coordinate, implement, and monitor the objectives outlined in this Plan. The CPSG will continue to assess methods, expenditures, and agency activities to reduce risk and protect the maritime industry from piracy and related acts of maritime crime. The Departments of State, Defense, Homeland Security, Justice, Transportation, and the Treasury, and the Director of National Intelligence will contribute to, coordinate, and undertake initiatives to support this Framework within existing resources. The CPSG will provide recommendations to the National Security Council, through the Maritime Security Interagency Policy Committee, to update this policy when conditions in Somalia change.

Framework for Combating Piracy and Enhancing Maritime Security in the Gulf of Guinea

---

Background

Piracy and related maritime crime in the Gulf of Guinea (GOG), a strategically significant region of Africa, are increasingly placing at risk the interests of the United States and our allies and partners. These maritime crimes threaten to undermine the four pillars of the *U.S. Strategy Toward Sub-Saharan Africa*, which include spurring broad-based and inclusive economic growth, trade, and investment, as well as advancing peace and security. Hijackings for fuel and cargo oil theft constitute the majority of incidents, though there are also significant numbers of robberies and kidnappings for ransom (KFR). These maritime attacks largely occur in weakly governed territorial seas that extend as far west as Cote d'Ivoire and as far south as Gabon.

The GOG suffers from a combination of factors that make it vulnerable to piracy, robbery at sea, and related maritime crime that are far more complex and violent than that occurring on the east coast of Africa. Many countries in the GOG region have ineffective governance, weak rule of law, precarious legal frameworks, inadequate naval, coast guard, and maritime law enforcement forces, and corrupt systems of government. While crude oil theft has been an issue for many years in the Niger Delta, recent hijackings of tankers transporting refined petroleum products and the increase in kidnappings for ransoms off the Niger Delta are of growing concern for both mariners and the oil industry operating in the region. When maritime criminals focus on the high value cargo aboard oil tankers and general cargo vessels, with little regard for the operators, it becomes much more dangerous for mariners.

Criminals can only thrive in areas where they operate with impunity either due to inadequate criminal justice systems or governments that are susceptible to corruption. For many people in the GOG, including the most powerful individuals, illicit markets present opportunities for personal enrichment not found in the legal economy with low risk of negative consequences. Partnerships with politically committed stakeholders, like the Economic Communities of West and Central African States, are critical to reducing opportunities for maritime crime and piracy within the GOG. Nigeria has the largest regional economy, and its potential willingness to institute rule of law and effective governance will reflect much of what can be achieved by the entire region.

The maritime sector is fundamental to a State's national defense, law enforcement, economy, and social goals and objectives. Africa's seas, lakes, and rivers are crucial sources of livelihood, as well as food and water security for many communities. These water sources also serve as a platform for trade and commerce (including for landlocked countries), as a theater for potential conflict, and, if poorly governed, as an area that transnational criminal networks can exploit with impunity. Investors are less inclined to do business in risky environments due to the increased cost of operating in higher crime areas. The absence of effective maritime governance dissuades capital investment, discourages growth, threatens food security, and hinders a State's ability to improve the conditions that contribute to its citizens' quality of life. This leads to increases in other areas of maritime crime, such as illegal, unreported, and unregulated fishing; human trafficking; the smuggling of narcotics; and circumventing sanctions through the shipment of contraband goods and weapons. In contrast, improved levels of maritime security enable a State to more effectively detect, deter, and interdict illicit actors whose actions indirectly or directly challenge local governance, health, and stability. Improvements in governance promote stability and encourage the growth of commerce within those nations that enforce rule of law.

The United States and partner nations play a leading role in western Africa's oil sector, which provides high-quality, light-sweet oil, and is important to the region's economy. Nigeria, Gabon, Ghana, and other countries around the GOG produce more than 3 million barrels of oil a day, or about one-third of Africa's output. Nigeria and Equatorial Guinea are also leading liquefied natural gas exporters. Oil output disruptions in West Africa could affect global oil prices, including within the United States, due to strong interconnectedness within the international market. Seafarers are becoming increasingly wary of using the seas in the GOG as the number of acts of piracy, armed robbery at sea, and related maritime crime rises. The United States must continue to partner with member states in the GOG to increase maritime security capacity, forge a concerted effort to stem piracy and armed robbery at sea, and prevent the region from becoming susceptible to the same conditions associated with the Horn of Africa.

The foundation for expanding maritime security in the GOG exists within strategies recently developed by African nations. The 2050 African Integrated Maritime Strategy (2050 AIMS), which was adopted at the 22nd Annual African Union (AU) Summit in January 2014, provides member States with many ambitious goals, including a regional vision that establishes a "Blue Economy"[1] in African waters before 2050. West and Central African nations signed a Code of Conduct[2] in Yaoundé in June 2013 that will be instrumental in enforcing maritime law. The International Maritime Organization (IMO) also supports the efforts of Economic Community of Central African States (ECCAS) and the Economic Community of West African States (ECOWAS) in its strategy, *Implementing Sustainable Maritime Security Measures in West and Central Africa.*

Overview of the Threat

Maritime crimes targeting high-value asset operations in the GOG emerged as a regional problem in the late 1990s. Since then, the incidence of piracy and armed robbery at sea in the GOG has waxed and waned, but has remained a concern for the shipping and energy industries, as well as for regional states and their trading partners. As of 2014, armed criminals, primarily based out of Nigeria, generally steal cargoes consisting of refined oil or other products. Unlike piracy off the Horn of Africa, the Nigerian criminals have no safe place to keep captured ships while negotiating ransoms. Generally speaking, there are three types of incidents in the GOG–low-level robberies, kidnap for ransoms, and hijacking for cargo theft. Although most attacks continue to happen inside territorial seas, many attacks occur beyond 12 nautical miles and often beyond the range of navies in the region. The overall number of attacks remains very difficult to

---

[1] The 2050 AIMS defines "Blue Economy" as an approach that "improves African citizens well-being while significantly reducing marine environmental risks as well as ecological and biodiversity deficiencies."
[2] Code of Conduct Concerning the Repression of Piracy, Armed Robbery Against Ships, and Illicit Maritime Activity in West and Central Africa, 2013.

gauge because incidents often go unreported. The attacks damage Nigeria's lucrative oil industry as the hijackings of product tankers increase the risk of doing business in the country. Estimates indicate that the country is losing approximately $1.5 billion a month to maritime crime, which includes piracy, armed robbery at sea, smuggling, and bunkering fraud, and its production is 400,000 barrels below its capacity of 2.5 million barrels per day.

Criminal groups that conduct KFR in Nigeria typically target small tug and supply vessels, and these groups are likely operating separately and independently from the fuel-theft networks likely based in Lagos. All of the reported KFR incidents around the GOG have occurred off the Niger Delta region.

In the GOG, maritime criminals are able to take advantage of a well-established illicit and corrupt political economy, as well as a lack of consistent and effective governance in the maritime domain. Criminals in this region maintain access to established international criminal networks and close ties to the shipping industries. Consequently, attacks are better coordinated than off the Horn of Africa, executed with precision, and often impossible to trace. West Africa's criminal organizations have deep international ties, and the trends indicate an increased willingness for criminal gangs to venture further from their shore-side bases to commit their crimes.

On average, there are 12 to 15 GOG port calls a year by U.S.-flagged, deep draft cargo ships. Approximately 70 U.S.-registered Offshore Supply Vessels (OSVs) are working out of Nigerian and Ghanaian ports supporting offshore oil exploration. Both types of vessels carry crews that may include U.S. citizens. In addition, there are numerous vessels operating in the GOG and engaged in coastwise trade, which requires operating in territorial seas and coastal waters and making frequent port calls in the region. An unknown number of U.S. mariners work aboard these vessels, as well as on cargo ships, tankers, and OSVs flagged in other nations operating in the region. The escalation in violent criminal activities will increasingly put U.S. citizens in harm's way and has already required the expenditure of significant resources to resolve hostage situations.

The pattern of piracy and related maritime crime also raises an increasing concern due to the violence associated with hijackings. In its 2014 report on piracy and armed robbery at sea, the International Maritime Bureau warns of the dangers to ships transiting West African waters, particularly around Nigeria, Benin, and Togo, and urges heightened vigilance, drawing particular attention to the expansion of the danger region. In 2013, the number of Nigerian criminal maritime attacks grew and currently stands at its highest level since 2008. Nigerian criminals accounted for 31 of the 51 attacks reported in the region in 2013, and West Africa, as a whole, saw 19 percent of attacks worldwide last year. The increase in maritime attacks in West Africa led London-based Lloyd's Market Association, an umbrella group of maritime insurers, to list Nigeria, Benin, and nearby waters in the same risk category as Somalia. The result was a significant decrease in maritime traffic in the region, which led to a substantial loss in revenue for regional nations and significant impact on the livelihoods of the country's citizens through an increase in the cost of imports and a decrease in the competitiveness of exports.

The nature of the attacks, porous borders, limited maritime law enforcement and interdiction assets, endemic corruption, and lack of political will allow criminal gangs to carry out fast attacks with the ability to quickly return to shore and avoid detection and capture. In addition, a high number of attacks are widely believed to be unreported due to an ongoing failure by regional States to pursue criminal action, complicity by law enforcement officials, and a desire to keep insurance rates low.

Objectives

The paramount goal of the United States is to safeguard U.S. citizens and U.S. interests, including protecting the lawful flow of commerce in the GOG. This will best be accomplished in the maritime domain by reducing corruption, increasing the political will, and developing the capacity and coordination of regional maritime authorities in the GOG to patrol and monitor illicit activity effectively and provide sufficient protection of vessels conducting lawful commerce. Although the underfunding of the maritime sector by regional states will present near-term challenges, a continued focus on the link between economic development and maritime security provides the best prospect for a sustainable approach. The United States, in concert with partner nations, international coalitions, and nongovernmental organizations, will continue to focus on the three primary areas of prevention, response, and governance. U.S. departments and agencies, consistent with respective authorities and other national missions and priorities, will pursue the following objectives.

Prevention of Attacks

The regional community, despite its efforts to increase coordination and capacity, is not yet able to patrol the entire region in the GOG effectively. Actions by industry and merchant mariners are critical in protecting cargo and preventing the capture of merchant mariners and commercial vessels in high-risk waters. Techniques to hinder and prevent maritime criminals continue to be the best method for increasing security and safety of mariners.

- Inform U.S. citizens. Maritime Advisories and Port Security Advisories, which clearly outline regional threats, continue to provide critical guidance on best management practices to protect U.S. merchant mariners, ships, and cargo in the GOG. U.S. departments and agencies will work with public-facing elements of the United States Government, such as the Department of State's Bureau of Consular Affairs, the U.S. Coast Guard, and the Department of Transportation, to provide timely threat assessments and warnings for U.S. citizens and companies traveling through or working in the GOG.

- Increase the risk to criminals operating in the maritime domain. Develop ECCAS-ECOWAS best practices to increase the consequences for criminals attempting attacks. Promote an increase in regional naval and law enforcement presence in the region to serve as a strong deterrent and quick response to maritime attacks.

- Seek industry partnership. The United States Government will continue to engage the shipping industry to provide input, follow best management practices, and require U.S.-

flagged vessels to implement effective measures to protect against pirates and armed robbers operating at sea.

- Track Privately Contracted Armed Security Personnel (PCASP). The Department of State, in coordination with other interagency partners, will continue to track the regional States' procedures or restrictions for the use of PCASP in order to be able to provide current information for U.S. shipping interests.

- Pursue the implementation of international standards for PCASP, which include an integrated approach to security, planning, training, awareness, documentation, and communication skills. GOG nations have strongly resisted including PCASP within their territorial seas. The United States and maritime partners must respect the sovereignty of these nations, while also demonstrating the benefits of well-trained PCASP in increasing maritime security and lawful commerce.

- Assist in the development of enhanced regional maritime patrols. Although GOG States prohibit, to varying degrees, the use of PCASP (including the import and export of weapons and equipment), there remains a need for enhanced security in these more dangerous territorial seas. Within the territorial seas of GOG nations, the marine industry must rely on the maritime security capabilities of the regional States. Most of these nations often lack resources and trained personnel; in addition, corrupt officials may be complicit in and actively encouraging maritime attacks. To protect mariners, the United States should promote - and assist in strengthening - the concept of armed convoys and/or regional maritime patrols to increase sustainability and effectiveness.

Respond to Acts of Maritime Crime

Building on the successful efforts against piracy and armed robbery at sea, the United States will continue to provide naval and law enforcement presence when available, and build capacity with regional nations to combat maritime crimes and facilitate lawful commerce within the GOG. Enhanced capabilities will strengthen partner nations' capacities to exercise their authorities and responsibilities to deter, detect, and interdict unlawful acts, such as the illicit movement of people, drugs, arms, and money. Increased capacity also enables governments to support other at-sea governance concerns including the ability to provide assistance to preserve the safety of life at sea and address the welfare of maritime migrants, including refugees and asylum seekers.

- Strengthen regional maritime capacity. The GOG will continue to be a priority area for U.S. security assistance. U.S. maritime-sector assistance should be provided in a multi-national setting with other international partners, when possible, and focused on regional engagement built on strong partnerships with key countries. The United States Government trains, equips, and conducts exercises and operations with African maritime forces through programs like Africa Partnership Station, which is conducted cooperatively with our international partners. The United States should investigate providing excess defense articles to nations that have the capacity to absorb increased capability and demonstrate resolve and commitment to countering piracy and related maritime crime. The United States will reinforce the importance of port security, as a key component of maritime security, and provide advice on implementing all aspects of the International Ship and Port Facility Security Code.

- Expand combined operations with African partners. The primary reason U.S. warships are operating in the region is to support capacity-building efforts. Consistent with other U.S. mission requirements and priorities, the United States should continue to conduct the African Maritime Law Enforcement Partnership (AMLEP) mission. A valuable partnership and capability building mechanism, AMLEP focuses on partner nation jurisdiction and criminal justice sector capability to identify areas where additional capacity building would strengthen the entire interdiction and enforcement continuum. AMLEP has contributed significantly to establishing more effective maritime security operations off the coasts of Senegal, The Gambia, and Cabo Verde. Many of the lessons learned in these nations can be applied throughout the GOG. Ghana, Togo, Benin, and Nigeria are priority countries for future AMLEP expansion, followed by Cameroon, Gabon, Cote d'Ivoire, and Sao Tome and Principe.

- Reinforce the longstanding U.S. policy of discouraging the payment of ransom, prisoner release, policy changes, or other acts of concession. The payment of ransom emboldens criminal enterprises and does little to deter future acts of piracy or kidnapping.

- Facilitate the development of an integrated strategy among all GOG nations to enhance intelligence and information sharing, training, assets, surveillance, and maintenance, and increase their ability to control waters. The development of shared maritime domain awareness, including both enhanced capability and operational coordination mechanisms, pursuant to a regional framework, will increase synergy and transparency in combating piracy, armed robbery at sea, and related maritime crime.

- Support the development of operational planning by key countries, such as Nigeria, Ghana, and Cameroon. The efficient use of available resources, such as placing patrol boats at key strategic chokepoints and conducting random boardings, will inhibit kidnappers and other organized criminals from deploying from, and returning to, safe havens. The United States will support efforts by Nigeria to enforce land-based security in the Niger Delta and reduce strongholds for maritime criminals.

- Lead regional operations and training exercises, in coordination with international partners, to develop competencies with regional navies and coast guards. Several nations in the region, which have limited maritime crime in their territorial seas, possess great potential to share lessons learned through successful training programs and capable interdiction operations. The United States and international partners should expand naval security training (focusing on anti-piracy), including tracking, interdicting, seizing, and prosecuting criminals.

- Encourage nations to implement the Code of Conduct[3] and pursue regional integration. Critical progress can be made in the development of domestic laws and regulations that criminalize piracy and related maritime crime, coupled with joint maritime interdiction operations and enhanced judicial systems.

- Develop regional capability to conduct law enforcement investigations. Analysis of crime scenes following piracy and violent attacks, including the collection of forensic evidence and case package development, will increase the success of pursuing and prosecuting leaders of criminal enterprises.

Enhance Maritime Security and Governance

Defeating piracy and related maritime crime requires functional governments with the political will to pursue and prosecute all levels within criminal enterprises. Maritime crime flourishes under complicit governance and is limited under effective rule of law. Absent strong commitment and action from local governments, there is little reason to believe that attacks in the GOG will decline. Therefore, the United States, along with our international partners, will advise and facilitate the development of regional governance, enhance political will to combat these crimes, develop key institutions to prosecute perpetrators, and support increased economic development.

- Strengthen the judicial sector. This includes strengthening the broad array of civil and criminal justice-related activities required to support rule of law and compliance in the maritime domain. In addition to the relevant customary international law on piracy reflected in the 1982 Law of the Sea Convention, the 1979 Hostage Taking Convention, the 1988 Convention on the Suppression of Unlawful Acts Against the Safety of Maritime Navigation, the 2000 Transnational Organized Crime Convention, and the 1999 Terrorist Financing Convention may apply to piracy cases in some circumstances. We will fully support and encourage the appropriate exercise of jurisdiction over interdicted pirates in accordance with relevant international law.

- Build political will and strategic frameworks. The United States will continue to support ECCAS and ECOWAS in their effort to develop regional frameworks for maritime cooperation. The United States has supported the organizations and its member states in drafting the signed ECCAS-ECOWAS Memorandum of Understanding and a Code of Conduct for Central and West Africa. Further support will be necessary in supporting the regional bodies and member states in their effort to draft and execute an implementation plan for the frameworks. The United States should also continue its support to ECOWAS and member States on their effort to implement the ECOWAS Integrated Maritime Strategy and establish a pilot maritime Zone E (Nigeria, Benin, Togo, and Niger).

---

[3] Code of Conduct Concerning the Repression of Piracy, Armed Robbery Against Ships, and Illicit Maritime Activity in West and Central Africa, 2013.

- <u>Strengthen information sharing.</u> The United States Government will encourage and support the Maritime Trade Information Sharing Center – Gulf of Guinea (MTISC-GOG) in Accra, Ghana. The MTISC-GOG aims to improve the regional maritime domain picture, analyze the information received, and share the information with regional maritime operations centers and industry vessels and production facilities in the GOG. Additionally, U.S. support to regional and national maritime operation centers will facilitate greater information sharing and improve operational standards.

- <u>Support the capacity of States' in the region to address the impunity for those actors conducting or facilitating piracy and related maritime crime.</u> The GOG Code of Conduct includes a commitment from signatory States to ensure persons committing or attempting to commit a transnational crime in the maritime domain are apprehended and prosecuted. Where appropriate, the United States Government will help our African partners build their capacity to investigate and prosecute cases effectively. Two potential focus areas are the States' ability to collect forensics evidence from the ships after an attack, and coordination among law enforcement, navies, and prosecutors.

- <u>Promote sustainable, broad-based, and inclusive maritime economic development</u>. Inequitable distribution of benefits from marine resources – such as fisheries, minerals, oil, and gas – poses serious threats to peace and security in Africa. Inclusive economic growth will ensure that benefits are broadly distributed in an open, transparent, and participatory approach. The United States will focus on improving: science-based decisionmaking processes; integration of human-built and natural infrastructure to maintain ecosystem goods and services upon which many vulnerable coastal communities depend; maintenance of critical habitats for cost-effective coastal adaption and resilience; a modern marine transportation system; and support for capacity building and regulatory focus for sustainable management of maritime revenue streams from tourism, fishing, resource extraction, commercial shipping, and port operations. The United States Government will continue to encourage Nigerian government representatives to work closely with civil society to address systemic problems related to maritime security.

- <u>Strengthen the Africa Constituency</u>. Additional efforts to develop an Africa constituency will support and enable stakeholders (coastal communities, civil society, private sector, academic, media, commerce, scientific, etc.) to engage in the decision-making process over marine resource use, benefit equitably from these resources and maritime commerce, access reliable data and information as it relates to maritime issues, and generate a demand for strong maritime security.

- <u>Promote accountable, transparent, and responsive governance</u>. The United States will support and empower key reformers and institutions of government at all levels to promote the rule of law; strengthen checks on executive power; incorporate responsive governance practices; enhance transparent accounting of oil-related sales; transfers, and investments; develop policies to strengthen maritime security; and improve decision-making processes at national and local levels, including specific maritime, commercial, regulatory, and/or criminal justice institutions. The United States also will emphasize to key nations that complicity in oil theft leads to increased instability and reduced profits for the entire nation.

- Use strategic communications to maintain political momentum and action by the African regional organizations and their member states. The United States Government will seek bilateral and multilateral opportunities to emphasize the need for good maritime governance and action to hold individuals accountable for acts of piracy and related maritime crime.

Partnerships

International cooperation and integration among regional nations, international organizations, industry, and other entities that have an interest in maritime security is necessary to ensure the full range of lawful and timely actions to combat piracy and related maritime crime in the GOG.

Most of the world's maritime domain is not subject to the sovereignty or jurisdiction of any single State, and many States do not have the capability or capacity to protect commercial shipping on the high seas, or even within their own territorial seas. International coalitions and partner nations that provide maritime patrol forces contribute to reducing, but cannot provide a complete response to, this threat. An effective response to piracy and armed robbery at sea requires coordinated and comprehensive multilateral and multi-sectorial cooperation on a global scale with regional focus.

Cooperation in the GOG between the coastal regional governments occurs through ECOWAS and ECCAS. U.N. Security Council Resolutions 2018 (2011) and 2039 (2012) noted that States in the region have a leadership role to play and the international community should assist in strengthening their efforts. This was supported in August 2013 when the U.N. Security Council released a presidential statement recognizing "the primary responsibility of [regional] States in the eradication of piracy and armed robbery at sea." Although the political will and regional cooperation are limited within the GOG, nations have the capability to govern and control their territorial seas.

Established in 2013, and as an outcome of the U.S.-hosted November 2012 G-8++ Africa Clearinghouse, the G-8++ Friends of Gulf of Guinea (FOGG) serves as the primary international coordination body on GOG maritime security. The FOGG meets on a biannual basis with a focus on donor coordination to improve the collective goal of sustainable capacity building. Participation to date has included the AU, Australia, Belgium, Brazil, Canada, Denmark, ECOWAS, ECCAS, the European Union, France, Germany, Interpol, Italy, Japan, the Netherlands, Norway, Portugal, Russia, Spain, the United Kingdom, the United Nations Office of Drugs and Crime (UNODC), and the United States. The United States actively participates in the G-8++ FOGG. The first G-8++ FOGG meeting in the GOG region was held in November 2013.

We continue to work with our international partners to strengthen collective lines of effort. Working in coordination with France and the United Kingdom, the United States developed a G-8++ matrix to help coordinate international activities in the region, which is based on the U.S. Maritime Security Sector Reform Guide. The United States is also leading an effort, in coordination with the United Kingdom, France, the European Union, UNODC, and Interpol, to develop a joint strategy to address impunity of those who commit acts of piracy and related maritime crime in the GOG by focusing on the elements necessary for States to prosecute the criminals effectively.

Industry, a primary contributor to the development of the economy in the region, plays a large role in partnerships against piracy and related maritime crime. As a key component in the economic engine, independent oil companies should be encouraged to partner with nations that support transparency and cultivate responsibility in promoting safety and security at sea. Industry will naturally increase investments where risk remains low. The United States should continue to partner with industry to support maritime law enforcement efforts.

Implementation, Monitoring, and Review

A strategic milestone will be the development of an implementation plan for the GOG Code of Conduct by the African partners. The operationalization of Zone E by Togo, Benin, and Nigeria will also demonstrate the level of political will and capacity to regionalize the African response to the piracy and armed robbery threat. An increase in investigating and prosecuting cases and a reduction in the trend of piracy and related maritime crime will also serve as a tangible indicator of successful implementation of this Plan. Consideration of intangible benefits may also be evaluated through the Maritime Security Sector Reform Guide created jointly by the Departments of State, Defense, Homeland Security, Transportation, and Justice and the U.S. Agency for International Development.

The Counter Piracy Steering Group (CPSG), consisting of a high-level interagency working group led by the Departments of State and Defense, will coordinate, implement, and monitor the objectives outlined in this Plan. The CPSG shall continue to assess methods and agency activities to reduce risk and protect the maritime industry from acts of piracy and related maritime crime.

The Departments of State, Defense, Commerce, Energy, Homeland Security, Justice, Transportation, and the Treasury, and the U.S. Agency for International Development and the Director of National Intelligence will contribute to, coordinate, and undertake initiatives in support of this Framework within existing resources. United States Government departments and agencies will coordinate activities, design sustainable solutions to maritime security based on a comprehensive and multi-dimensional approach, and support, as feasible, African-led and owned maritime security initiatives. The CPSG will provide recommendations to the National Security Council, through the Maritime Security Interagency Policy Committee, to update this policy when conditions in the GOG change.